i

Extreme Money Makeover

Extreme Money Makeover

Oscar & Crystal Jones

Destiny House Publishing, LLC
Detroit, MI

Extreme Money Makeover

Published by Destiny House Publishing, LLC
Copyright 2010 Oscar & Crystal Jones
International Standard Book Number:

Original printing November 2010
Cover design and Publication Layout:
Destiny House Publishing, LLC

Printed in the United States of America

For information: Destiny House Publishing, LLC
P.O. Box 19774 Detroit, MI 48219
www.destinyhousepublishing.com
888.890.4555

Extreme Money Makeover

Contents

Acknowledgments

We acknowledge our Lord and Savior,
Jesus Christ:

Thank you, Lord, for giving us the financial
wisdom to experience an extreme money
makeover. We love you and appreciate all
that you are to us.

Dedications

We dedicate this book to
Our wonderful children:

Jake & Keila,
Kyria,
Charity & Erik,
LaTina,
and Christopher

And to our amazing grandchildren:
Kristin, Arielle, Jaiman, and Elijah

We love you and pray for you fervently. We
believe that as you completely surrender your
lives to the Lord, you will begin your journey
to an extreme money makeover.

Introduction

God has given you ideas. He gives you big ideas. And sometimes the idea is so big, you get intimidated. You can become paralyzed by it because it's so huge. Too often, we sit and do nothing. And someone else picks it up and runs with it. They grab the wealth. And we wind up sitting somewhere kicking ourselves, sadly recounting to others how we thought of it first.

Thinking about it, is not enough. You must do something with your thoughts. Bring them from the spiritual realm into the natural realm. Every successful business, invention, book, started as an idea. Get it out of your head and into your hands.

If you ask God for the wealth, you had better understand its purpose. Your first priority is to seek the kingdom. Matthew 6:33 says, "Seek ye first the kingdom of God and His righteousness and all these things will be added unto you." What things? The things that Matthew describes are our basic necessities. Your focus should not be the clothes, jewelry, houses, etc. Materialism should not become your God. As we seek God's mind and His perspective, He is able to make all things abound toward us.

Who qualifies for a makeover?

True wealth comes from God. True wealth encompasses every area of our life. We can have a fully prosperous life when we are connected to God. This includes wholesome thriving relationships, good health, right attitudes, proper habits, etc. This doesn't mean a person who doesn't serve God can't obtain riches. That would be an absurd thing to say. Wealth is for the promotion of God's kingdom. So while it's possible to obtain riches without God. Riches and wealth are not the same thing. And acquiring them involves different paths. Those who only want riches can do so without God. However it is God that gives us the power to get wealth. So those who want wealth must submit to the plan of God; walking in faith. It is much more effective to have God working on your behalf to produce enduring riches that will affect every area of your life.

Nevertheless, we must understand that doubt, fear, anger and unbelief handcuffs God from working in our lives. These spirits will always cause us to complain. "Why doesn't God come through for me?" "Why are other people prospering and I am not?" "Nothing good ever comes to me". "I've tried faith and it just doesn't work."

A complaining spirit provokes God. There is absolutely NO benefit to walking in these spirits. It only makes you feel worse. You aren't as productive. You become stifled in your creativity. You can't hear God. You can't please God. You can't move forward. The Bible tells us not to forget God's benefits. Write down all His benefits, blessings and favor that you have received in your life. Meditate on them. Praise Him for them. Do not concentrate on the obstacle, trial, or circumstance that is present in your situation. Focus on God's ability. There is nothing He can't handle.

Chapter 1

What is an Extreme Money Makeover?

What is an extreme money makeover? It is a radical economical transformation that begins with the way we think about wealth. When we have the right perspective about wealth, our lives will be revolutionized.

An extreme money makeover involves a paradigm shift. Paradigm is defined as the framework for a person's belief system founded on our culture and environment. A paradigm shift is a transformation from one way of thinking to another. Most often this shift is dramatic or drastic; which is why we call it extreme.

It is a revolution. A paradigm shift does not evolve or simply happen. It is sparked. It is driven by extreme desire.

The purpose of this book is to ignite something in you. We expect to stretch your thinking. We hope to challenge your mindset and thereby change your life and livelihood. When you are done, we hope that you will dream bigger and clearer. You will dream in vivid living color. You will reach for that which has been deemed impossible and out of reach. You will see things that you've never been able to see before.

It is our aim to cause the people of God to enlarge their territories. We encourage you to grow your thinking so large that you surprise yourself.

This book could have been entitled Extreme Wealth Makeover. It is more than about money. Money is a byproduct of living a wealthy life. We define wealthy as the highest level of living; prosperous. We should have prosperous relationships, attitudes, health, ministries and finances.

Therefore this makeover is essential for the believer. God requires that we all shift. He wants us to embrace God-sized and God-shaped thinking. Forsake the ordinary and average for something more.

> I am come, that they might have life,
> and that they might have it more
> abundantly. St. John 10:10b

> Beloved, I wish above all things that
> thou mayest prosper and be in health,
> even as thy soul prospereth.III John 2:1

Some of us have always sensed that we were created for something more; something bigger than ourselves. We confirm that for you. It is true. It's time to leave that small, *barely enough* mindset. God has grand things in store for His people. Let Him take you on the adventure of an amazing lifetime.

Now is your time. Reach. Stretch. Pull. Expand. Arise. The Greater One lives inside of you. He is able to do exceeding, abundantly above all that we ask or think *according to the power that works in us. It's time to unleash that power that works in us.* God has empowered a chosen people to expand His kingdom.

Get ready, get set, grow.

Chapter 2

It's Time to Shift

Essential to any makeover is the tearing down of the old. The thought patterns that got us where we are today must be excavated. It's time for old things to pass away. All things must be made new. We must do something different, in order to get something different.

When our minds or hearts have been renovated, then our words will change. Out of the abundance of the heart, the mouth speaks (Matthew 12:34). So if our hearts are filled with God's positive life-giving Word, that is what will come out of our mouths. As it comes out of our mouths, it will mold our lives. However, if our hearts are filled with negative, death sentencing words, than that will be the fruit of our lips. And those words will mold our lives. The scriptures warn us that life and death are in the power of the tongue (Proverbs 18:21).

What in the world are you saying?

> "I am broke." "I can't do it." "I will never make it."
> "I don't have what it takes." "I don't know how."
> "I don't have a degree." "People don't like me."

These words evolve out of a poverty stricken heart. What we speak is what we will draw into our lives. When you soak a sponge in vinegar, when it is squeezed, only what's in it will come out of it. What are you soaking your sponge in?

We ought to fill our hearts with God's Word, so that the right things come out.

A good person produces good things from

the treasury of a good heart, and an evil person produces evil things from the treasury of an evil heart. What you say flows from what is in your heart. Luke 6:45 NLT

So it is important that we store God's word in our hearts. His word is key to our success.

Finally brethren, whatsoever things are true, whatsoever things are honest, whatsoever things are just, whatsoever things are pure, whatsoever things are lovely, whatsoever things are of good report; if there be any virtue, and if there be any praise, think on these things. Philippians 4:8

For as he thinketh in his heart, so is he... Proverbs 23:7a

You are what you think you are.

We must understand the power of thoughts and words. Too often, we minimize them. We allow ourselves to say and think anything that comes to us. We meditate on negative issues, not fully realizing that we are forming our future.   We are where we are today because of our thoughts and words from the past. The scriptures tell us to cast down imaginations, to take captive every thought that exalts itself against what you know about Christ. We must be aware of how serious this is; because our negative thinking cancels our faith. The Word warns us that we cannot please God if faith is absent from our lives. Faith is not for some future time.

Faith is for your present situation. It is for your "now". Faith allows the invisible to become visible. Faith looks at God and his abilities and strengths. Fear and negativity look at self in its limitations.

We serve a boundless God. We must always look to him in expectation. We can do all things through Christ which strengthens us.

Therefore, we must do something with those negative thoughts that surface. Don't embrace them. Don't receive them. Don't act on them. Reject any and every thought that does not line up with the Word of God.

What are you thinking? Your thoughts will become your words. What are you speaking? Your words will become your life. By your words are you justified and by your words are you condemned.

God has our very best interest at heart. He delights in seeing his children prosper.

> Let them shout for joy, and be glad, that favour my righteous cause: yea, let them say continually, Let the Lord be magnified, which hath pleasure in the prosperity of his servant. Psalm 35:27

The Lord means us good and not evil. He has a wonderful future in store for us. When our thoughts match God's thoughts of us, we will see transformation.

> For I know the thoughts that I think toward you, saith the Lord, thoughts of peace, and not of evil, to give you to an expended end. Jeremiah 29:11

His desire is to lavishly bless those that belong to Him.

> …no good thing will he withhold from them that walk uprightly. Psalm 84:11b

> Beloved, I would above all things that you
> prosper in and be in health even as your
> soul prospers. III John 1:2

When we **really** know this, passed just being able to quote the scriptures, then our lives will be made over. God is glorified when His children prosper. He wills to bless us. God is not against us. He is for us. And if God is for us who can prosper against us? No one and no thing. His thoughts are of abundance, health and favor upon those that are His.

If we want to obtain the wealth that God has in mind for us, we must think scripturally. We must speak the Word. We must not allow ourselves to think or speak otherwise.

It is imperative that we cultivate a wealthy mindset. Then wealth will flow to us. The way we think about prosperity is critical to not only receiving the triumphant life but being able to hold on to it.

> Let the words of my mouth and the medi-
> tation of my hearts be acceptable in thy
> sight, o Lord, my strength and my
> redeemer. Psalms 19:14

You must think what He thinks. Say what He says. Repeat kingdom words. Declare them over your life. As a man thinks in his heart so is he. And whatever is in his heart is what he speaks. His speech becomes his life's path.

Words are spirit. They are alive and active. And they go forth in the earth to accommodate our declaration. Think about this:

> In the beginning, God created the heaven
> and the earth. And the earth was without
> form and void; and darkness was upon the

face of the deep. And the spirit of God moved upon the face of the waters. And God said, "Let there be light: and there was light. Genesis 1:1-3

And God said, …and there was. Powerful.   These are lively words.   In the midst of darkness and nothingness, God speaks. When God speaks, all of creation must line up with what has been spoken. He speaks a thing and it rushes into existence. He says it, and it happens.

God said, let there be light and there was light. God said, let there be a firmament in the heavens and there was a firmament. God said, let the waters under the heaven be gathered together unto one place and it was so. He continued to speak until the entire world was formed. When God spoke, everything in the atmosphere obeyed.

The only creation that does not obey God is man. Every planet, tree, wind, body of water, animal, insect and flower obeys God. The scripture says that if we don't give him praise, even the rocks will cry out. Our God is mighty and sovereign.   When He speaks something, it will simply happen. If God says, "The sky is green." Know that God has not lied or made a mistake. All of creation will begin working and the sky will obey. If you take a second look, the sky will turn green.

In the midst of the storm, Jesus spoke to the tumultuous winds and waves. He spoke, "Peace, Be still". The winds and waves obeyed Him. If we, His creation, are formed in His image, then we have been extended this same power as we become His children.   A creative Father begats creative children.

It's in our spiritual genes. We, that have been born again, possess our Father's spiritual DNA. We, too, can cause things to come forth by the words in our mouths, because our Dad has given us dominion over the earth. Everything in the earth must follow our decree. God has not only demonstrated it for us, but He told us to speak to the situations that arise in our lives.

> Luke 17:6 And the Lord said, If ye had faith as a grain of mustard seed, ye might say unto this sycamine tree, Be thou plucked up by the root, and be thou planted in the sea; **and it should obey you**.

> Matthew 17:20b ...for verily I say unto you, If ye have faith as a grain of mustard seed, ye shall say unto this mountain, Remove hence to yonder place: and it shall remove; and **<u>nothing shall be impossible unto you</u>**.

He has empowered us to speak to trees and mountains. How much more to those obstacles that spring up in our lives? We all know that nothing is impossible for God. But the scriptures say nothing shall be impossible for you. We are created in his likeness.

> Ephesians 4:20 puts it this way; He can do exceeding abundantly above all that we ask or think, **according to the power that works in us.**

As believers, we often underestimate the force and authority that has been granted to us as the children of God. We have the power to trample on serpents and scorpions and over all the power of the devil. It is not by our own fleshly power or ability. For then we would have reason to fear. But it is His power. We can walk in this authority, because we are plugged into the right source.

Consistently in scripture, we are warned to be slow to speak. We must be careful of the words we release out of our mouths. We must align our words with God's Word. We must be deliberate and cautious about what we speak. We are delicate about how we handle electricity because of its power. It is the same carefulness we need to have toward our speech.

Negative words produce negative results. Positive words produce positive results. We must speak right words. Right words come from the scripture. We must learn to say what God says; agree with Him. If we speak out of our emotions or out of our opinion, it could be death to us. We must know that God is the Great One. He is Omnipotent, Omniscient, and Omnipresent. So everything must flow out of Him to us. We mess up when we rely on our own strength. If we dive into God's Word, fully understanding who He is, we will walk in full confidence. We only doubt when our eyes are on flesh. We must always look to the Author and Finisher of our faith. He has a magnificent future in store for us.

Chapter 3

My Purpose, My Passion

What has God called you to do? Why were you born? What is in your heart? If you do not know, you need to seek God about your purpose. Every man has a purpose for which he was born. And that purpose must somehow tie in to advancing God's Kingdom.

Unless we have a proper understanding of our purpose, we will never receive all that God intends. There is no point in gaining wealth for bragging rights or to lavish it upon ourselves. The Bible keeps it all in perspective.

> What would it profit a man to gain the whole world and lose his soul? Mark 8:36

We were created to give God glory. Everything we do in the kingdom, should give glory to our Father. Our purpose is directly linked to the kingdom of God.

> In the same way, let your light shine before men, that they may see your good deeds and praise your Father in heaven. Matthew 5:16 NIV

So how does wealth tie into this? It takes a healthy body, a wealthy attitude and a good deal of finances to reach out to the lost. God gives us the power to get wealth to establish his covenant on the earth. His covenant involves helping those in darkness come to the light.

In St. Matthew 31-36, we are reminded of what God expects.

> For I was hungry, and ye gave me food: I

was thirsty and ye gave me drink: I was a stranger and ye took me in. Naked, and ye clothed me: I was sick and ye visited me: I was in prison, and ye came unto me.

The church is expected to meet the needs of those that are less fortunate. So everything we do should be tied to advancing the kingdom whether directly or indirectly.

The early church took care of the needs of the poor. Somehow we've relinquished this important ministry to the government. The church at large has been guilty of spending so much time, money and thought on her own concerns that she has forgotten what her bridegroom asked her to do.

We have lost our zeal for true ministry. The Bible says, true religion is taking care of the widows and the orphans. Are we feeding the hungry? Are we concerned about the sick? When we are concerned, God will make sure we are supplied amply with the resources needed.

> A certain man went down from Jerusalem to Jericho, and fell among thieves, which stripped him of his raiment, and wounded him, and departed, leaving him half dead. And by chance there came down a certain priest that way: and when he saw him, he passed by on the other side. And likewise a Levite, when he was at the place, came and looked on him, and passed by on the other side. But a certain Samaritan, as he journeyed, came where he was: and when he saw him, he had compassion on him. And went to him, and bound up his wounds, pouring in oil and wine, and set him on his own beast, and brought him to an inn and took care of him. And on the

morrow when he departed he took out two pence, and gave them to the host, and said unto him, Take care of him; and whatsoever thou spendest more, when I come again, I will repay thee.
Luke 10:30-35

This is the story of the Good Samaritan. God gives us this as a model. This Samaritan paid this man's hospital bills. The two men weren't friends. In fact the Samaritan didn't even know this wounded soul. Yet, he had a heart of compassion. God is glorified in this. We are agents of the Lord. We are ambassadors for Christ. We are his hands, feet, and mouthpieces. We are the way God provides. Possessing wealth will allow us to give glory to our faithful Lord and complete our assignment on the earth.

Provision doesn't just drop out of the sky. If someone needs clothing, it doesn't fall from heaven. If a person is burned out of their home, God will call upon one of us. He keeps his covenant through our obedience. It's part of our purpose on the earth. What did Jesus tell us? If we feed the least of these, we have fed him. This is why we need the wealth. It is our holy duty. The purpose of all that God wants to put in your hands is to establish his covenant in the earth.

But thou shalt remember the LORD thy God: for it is he that giveth thee power to get wealth, that he may establish his covenant which he sware unto thy fathers, as it is this day. Deuteronomy 8:18

What is His covenant? He has made some promises to those that preceded us. He made promises to Abraham, Isaac and Jacob. He fulfilled some of those promises through the children of Israel. God's covenant also entails the list of promises to those that are in relationship with

Him as outlined in scripture. So consider this:

> Philippians 4:19 says, But my God shall
> supply all your need according to his
> riches in glory by Christ Jesus.

There is a reason for your prosperity. It's not just about
you. His plan is bigger than you. You must affect not just
your family, but your community. God is a promise
keeper. He must fulfill what he promised. He has made
promises to generations of believers. And He will use us
to fulfill those promises, if we allow Him.

A Methodist dentist processed the first bottles of
unfermented wine to use during his church's communion
service. Thomas wanted the church to stop using alcohol
during communion. Nevertheless his process was not
accepted by the church, initially. But his son, Charles,
eventually took over the business and caused it to prosper.
And he was able to financially support many missionaries
because of the success of his family's business, Welch's
Grape Juice.

So what is it that God has called you to do? Often we can
find our purpose in the thing we love to do and/or the place
of our intolerance. Perhaps you love to shop. Maybe God
will turn your shopping passion into a ministry: A Shop &
Share event for the needy. You may be intolerant of child
abuse or neglect. Your advocacy could prove to be your
ministry. If you love to cook, perhaps you will have a
feeding program for the homeless.

It's the passion that generates the wealth. So maybe your
passion is the thing that funds your call. Maybe your
passion is in construction. God can use you to finance an
orphanage or something totally disconnected to your call.
However you must understand what your call is and where
your passions lie.

Seek the Lord to find out what he is calling you to do. And you may be surprised to find the resources will follow. Money follows ministry.

Chapter 4

A Promised Inheritance

We have a promised inheritance. We are joint-heirs with Christ. When we refuse to prosper, we interfere with God's plan. If his children are in poverty, this doesn't benefit the kingdom. The kingdom is advanced by God's ambassadors. These are His sowers. Sowers will always be supplied with seed.

This is part of His covenant with us. He doesn't just drop provision out of the sky. He uses His people to fulfill His word. So the Lord may ask you to pay someone's light bill or buy them groceries. He may ask you to buy medicine for a senior citizen. Even more than that, some are called to build wells in third world countries. Others have a mandate to build orphanages in India. Some may be called to build hospitals, schools, churches, etc. in various communities around the globe.

> I have shewed you all things, how that so labouring ye ought to support the weak, and to remember the words of the Lord Jesus, how he said, It is more blessed to give than to receive.
> (Acts 20:35)

Therefore we become co-laborers with God in fulfilling His promise on the earth. It is our purpose to partner with Him. So it is imperative that we are able to stand in this offensive strategy of expressing obedience to God and love toward His people.

We need an ample amount of money to fully obey God in fulfilling our destiny. God tells us to pay our tithes and offerings to support the work (Proverbs 3:9).

He tells us to give to the poor (Proverbs 28:27), give to widows and orphans, (James 1:27, I Timothy 5:16), and give to our enemies (Proverbs 25:21), our government (Mark 12:17). He further instructs us to support the men and women of God who lead the church (I Timothy 5:18). He also tells us to help those in need (Proverbs 3:27-28). We are to do all these things all while not neglecting our financial duties to our families (I Timothy 5:8), and storing up for our grandchildren (Proverbs 13:22).

Whew! This is a big charge. These commands are laid on a Godly assumption that we have an abundant supply of money in which to fulfill these duties. God will never ask us to do something that we can't do. So, of course, we absolutely must have money. In fact, He goes on to say that the liberal soul shall be made fat (Proverbs11:25). The more we give, the more we will be blessed.

Money in and of itself will not make one rich. It's our thoughts that make us rich. If God cannot change your mind, he cannot prosper you. We must shed the poverty mentality and embrace a wealthy mindset. The wealthy mindset will cause a person to possess wealth. The poverty mindset will cause a person to have lack.

How many times have you heard stories of celebrities and athletes filing bankruptcy or dying with nothing left to their estates? There are countless stories of men and women who became millionaires overnight and one year later they had nothing to show for it. In fact, even those who win millions are usually worse off one year later than before they received the money. The problem is their minds had not changed. We must see ourselves the way that God sees us. And understand that victory is not dependent on us; but on God.

In Numbers 13 and 14, God had promised Israel, a wealthy land flowing with milk and honey. They sent spies to determine the strategy of taking the land. Ten of the spies brought back a negative word. The children of Israel refused to possess the promised wealth of God because of fear. They saw themselves as grasshoppers. Only 2 of them chose to believe God in the face of the enemy. Likewise, we see obstacles, so-called giants in our own lands. So we step back from what God asks. But if God says do it, we ought to do it. We must allow God to renew our minds. We must agree with Him. God wants to put finances in our hands. We ought to be distributors of His resources.

What does his covenant say to us? I will supply all your needs according to my riches. If he's going to supply the needs of His people, He needs to use us to receive the finances so that we can be the ones to distribute it. God uses people. So it is very necessary for us to gain wealth. It's not just for ourselves, but for others.

We are at times called upon to cover the basic needs of others. No believer should ever be without his/her medications because they can't afford it. God will call upon one or more of us to supply it. Believers are charged to depend on God and not the government.

Many times, not only are we unable to assist others, we can't even feed ourselves. As children of a prosperous Father, we should not live as paupers. We should have more than enough to do what God has asked us to do.

> The Lord is my Shepherd and I shall not
> lack. Psalm 23:1

Our basic necessities lack usually because of poor stewardship and unbelief. If a person does not pay tithes and offerings regularly, it demonstrates a lack of faith. And he/she will not have enough to make ends meet. We must not look through poverty-shaded lenses. We must see ourselves as providers instead of recipients, and as victors, not grasshoppers. We need to change the way we think. We need to accept the fact that God wants to funnel cash through us for His work. We must be willing to take what is in our hand and use it to the glory of the Father.

We are called to partner with God. He promises to prosper those that He can trust. He only trusts those that trust Him. We must use what he's given us to meet the needs of others.

Chapter 5

Poverty vs. Wealthy Spirit

A poverty spirit is self-centered. It is a spirit that looks internally at the needs of one - itself. A poverty spirit is one that rejoices in receiving more than in giving. The Bible tells us, clearly, that it is more blessed to give than to receive. The individual that operates in this spirit is always looking for others to give to him/her. It is unashamedly self-centered. We know that selfishness has no place in the kingdom. We must be others minded. A wealthy spirit looks externally at the needs of others.

The poverty spirit is often identified as stingy. A wealthy spirit can never attach itself to a poverty spirit. They are complete opposites. We must take a good honest look at ourselves. If we identify this spirit, we must work to rid ourselves of it. This is done by doing the opposite of what the flesh wants us to do. They that worship God must worship Him in spirit and in truth. So deny the complainer in yourself by praising. It is a spiritual act and operates in opposition to the flesh.

...But in lowliness of mind let each esteem other better than themselves. Look not every man on his own things, but every man also on the things of others.
Philippians 2:3b-4

The spirit of povery is an enemy to a wealthy spirit. You must look for it, to squash its operation in your life.

Poverty	Wealthy
Stingy/Selfish	Generous
Complainer	Praiser
Hoarder	Distributor
Fearful	Faithful
Self-pity	Compassion for others
Makes Excuses	Prays for answers
Procrastinator	Early bird
Suspicious	Trusting
Self-reliant	God-reliant
Beggar	Sower
Distracted	Focused
Disorganized	Orderly
Angry/bitter	Forgiving
Jealous of others	Celebrates others
Confusion	Peace
Lazy	Diligent

Do you recognize any traits of poverty working in your members? If so, you must allow your mind to be renewed. Study the scriptures on that area of poverty. When we get God's heart on it, we can respond properly to it.

If I study all the scriptures on complaining and murmuring, I wll find out how God looks at it. The scriptures tell us that murmuring provokes God to anger. An in-depth study will allow me to see how much God despises it. Therefore it will turn my heart to despise it, as well. This will cause me to shift to a wealthier mindset of praising, every time I think about complaining.

Poverty is a curse. God did not intend for us to live a miserable existence. We should have joy, peace, hope and clarity of vision and purpose. We should not be bitter and hateful. We will stifle our creativity. Neither should we live from paycheck to paycheck, barely making our bills. His plans for us are always much bigger than what we had in mind.   We cannot be content living a diminished lifestyle, full of chaos and lack. God has more for us. He did not call us to be a poverty minded people. We are favored as the people of God, chosen. We are set aside for His purpose. He says we are the head and not the tail, above only and not beneath. If we consider ourselves "the tail", or" beneath", we have poor thinking. We must <u>always</u> agree with God.

"Someday, I will…"   "When I have more money, I will…" These are excuses and symptoms of a poverty mindset. When we hear ourselves making excuses, it should alert us to shift our thinking. Every excuse can be overcome to those who possess a wealthy mindset.   The poverty minded sit down in the middle of excuses and throw emotional temper tantrums. The poverty spirit must always assign blame to someone. So tantrums are full of accusations against God. When we blame God, we are certainly not operating in faith. So God is not pleased.

A poverty spirit will shackle you to your oppositions. It refuses to allow you to move forward. However a wealthy mindset prays for solutions.   She/he looks for a way around the barrier. As the wealthy assesses the situation, he/she knows that the blockage is temporary. This is not the end. He whom the Son sets free is free indeed. Christ has set us free from every bondage. There is nothing we can't accomplish through Him.

Chapter 6

The Greatest Fear

The biggest hindrances to wealth are fear and intimidation. We become so paralyzed by the thought of failure, that it becomes a self-fulfilling prophecy. We fail because we talk ourselves into never getting started. Some get started but never complete anything. We sit down and give up in the midst of a bunch of unfinished projects.

Every journey begins with one step. But you will never get to your destination unless you **continue** to take those steps. You must see your God-given vision through to completion.

Fear in our culture is both caught and taught. We start out as babies unafraid of anything. That's why often it's easier to teach babies to swim than adults. Children are able to ice skate, do gymnastics, learn how to ski, etc. Because they are not yet convinced that they can't. Think about it. As toddlers, we didn't know limitations. We ventured into places that we shouldn't have. We put odd things into our mouths. We climbed the top of the monkey bars. We screamed in exuberance for our parents to watch as they squirmed with terror. We were oblivious to danger.

Children don't know fear until we teach it to them.

Have you ever seen a child hurt himself and get up laughing until he watches his parents panic? As we grow up, we pick up cues from our loved ones. We learn fear and limitations. And as we learn about danger, we learn and embrace fear. Our culture extracts our courage and sense of adventure. And we are taught that bad things happen when you go outside of the lines. And somehow the message sticks: Don't try anything, you might fail or get hurt.

Certainly we need wisdom. We don't just run out in front of cars. But somehow we must recapture our sense of freedom in order to launch out into the deep. We must be willing to try new things.

Our culture is continuously attempting to suck out our freedom and sense of God-adventure. We live in a world that is programmed to break our spirit. Ridicule and sarcasm abound. There are relatively few that will see what we are doing and tell us to go for it. We are in a world filled with competition and envy.

Consequently we not only fear failure, we fear rejection. We fear looking foolish in front of our peers. We fear disappointment. We fear success. We fear not knowing.

It should comfort us to know that God has not given us a spirit of fear. Fear comes from the evil one. God wants us to be fearless, completely trusting and relying on Him. He wants us to free fall into His arms with no inhibitions. He wants you to experience your life with an explanation mark. Really Live!

Suppose for a moment that there was no such thing as fear? What if nothing could hold you back? What is it that you would do? How would your life change? Who is this new person that you would become? Would you like yourself more? Stop here.

Take some time to answer these questions on paper. Don't rush past them. Carefully consider your answers. What would it be like to have a life with no fear? Do you want to find out? Are you ready to venture into a fearless future? Well, let's begin.

How do we get past the fear?

#1. Give yourself room to fail. *For a just man falleth seven times and riseth up again. Proverbs 24:16*

Dr. Seuss received numerous rejection letters before he ever sold his first book. Steven Jobs (CEO of Apple, Inc.) dropped out of college in his first semester.

It's not the end of the world if you fail attempting success. It is more problematic, if you fail because you never attempted anything. Too many dreams, ideas, inventions, and businesses end up in the grave. Fear robbed their owners of ever birthing them forth. Fear will cause you to miscarry the vision that God has given you. It is an enemy to your success.

You fell down many times as a baby before you learned to walk. Making mistakes is part of the process. When you allow yourself room to fail, you allow yourself room to do something great for the kingdom. None of us is perfect. God is fully aware of that. He gives us new mercy every morning. So grab hold of your new mercy and do something novel.

#2 Seek Knowledge. *And by knowledge all the chambers shall be filled with precious and pleasant riches.*
Proverbs 24:4

We live in the greatest time in history. The World Wide Web is a mega source of information. We've never had such easy access to so much information. We can find out basically anything, simply by typing in a question in a search engine. The vast majority of those facts are readily available at no cost. Maximize your use of this valuable resource. Search the web.

Talk to people in the area that you are interested in. Ask questions. Talk to experts. Find out what is needed. Spend time researching the idea that God has given you.

Know the pros and cons, strengths and weaknesses. Go into it fully armed with information. Sometimes we fear simply because we lack data. Dispel the fear. Seek the knowledge that you lack.

#3 Be open to the new. *Behold I will do a new thing now it shall spring forth; shall ye not know it? I will even make a way in the wilderness and rivers in the desert. Isaiah 43:19*

God does not always work in the same way. Be open to new ideas and new ways of doing things. Don't try to stuff this large God into a small box. It just won't work. He is innovative. He may give you an idea that makes no sense. Not long ago, the cell phone, electric car, iPod, iPad, eBooks, and the internet were things that didn't exist. And they may not have made sense to the average person. Today, it all does. Noah had to build the very first cruise ship. And it was enormous. Don't dismiss your idea because it's never been done. Do it!

Train yourself to be adventurous by trying something new at every opportunity. Go to new places. Try new routes. Take a class. Try a new dish. Step outside of routines. Unleash the adventurer in you. Your joy will be increased. Your excitement will be amplified.

#4 Be willing to start small. *Though thy beginning was small, yet thy latter end should greatly increase. Job 8:7.*

A slow or small start does not equal failure. Pace yourself. Don't expect to burst out of the gates. We aren't saying that you won't. However, it's not likely. There's a lot of value when success is slow and starts small.

A small start helps us with preparation and problem solving. Initially a few clients here and there will help tweak out trouble spots and prime you to be able to effectively handle the big accounts. He that is faithful over little will be ruler over much.

#5 Don't seek the approval of others. *We ought to obey God rather than man. Acts 5:29*

Follow God. It's okay to seek counsel. In fact, the Bible says in the multitude of counselors, there is safety. But if God has given you an idea, do not wait for others to approve of it. Most people will try to create your world a little smaller than their own. Let God cast your vision, not man.

#6 Do something. *Faith without works is dead, being alone. James 2:17*

We have no excuse for our excuses. It's time to put our faith in action and complete our assignment on earth. We must do something with our talents. One writer said that our talents are God's gifts to us, what we do with those talents are our gift to God.

It's time to activate our faith. Excuses are a refusal to prosper. Agree to do, say and go whatever and wherever God asks. It's good to have dreams. It's better to make those dreams a reality. There is no time like the present. Do something today to move into your wealthy place.

Chapter 7

Show Me the Money

The number one question on the heart of many believers is "Where is my money?" We have heard many people say, "I pay my tithes and offerings. Why don't I have my wealth?" We act as if the tithe alone is what unleashes a person's wealth. That's like saying, "Why isn't my car working? I put gas in it." There are many reasons why a person may not have achieved the wealth that God has in store for us. Each person must be surveyed separately. Many questions must be asked to get at the answer of the first. Below we've attempted to give a general assessment to get your vehicle of wealth in operation.

Are you walking in faith?

Complaining, fear, and doubt are signs that faith is not present. Without faith it is impossible to please God. We must first believe that He is God and secondly that He is a rewarder of those that diligently seek him. (Hebrews 11:6) Faith is key. Even in the face of adverse circumstances, we must keep the faith.

Are we paying tithes and offerings?

God tell us not to rob Him of the tithes and offerings (Malachi 3:8-12). We must give the tenth of our increase **and** a generous offering. God says that if we do so, He will open Heaven's window, and pour out a blessing to overflowing. He says we will have so much; there won't be room to receive it all. He promises to rebuke the devourer for our sakes. Our vine will yield at the proper time. All people will call us blessed. Wow! That is a wealthy place!

Sadly most of us do one or the other. We either tithe or give an offering. So we never experience the place of overflow. And many that do both, don't do it regularly. If we would just take God at his Word, we would experience His best. God's formula works. James Lewis Kraft of Kraft Foods, Inc. said it best, *"The only investment I ever made which has paid consistently increasing dividends is the money I have given to the Lord."*

Are you engaged in the work?

If a man doesn't work, he doesn't eat. God will prosper whatever is in our hands. He requires that we take the thing (the idea, the invention, the book, the product, etc.) and cast it upon the waters. He will bless the work of our hands. The "thing" doesn't have to be spiritual in nature. Paul made tents. Jesus was a carpenter. These natural gifts can help to financially undergird a spiritual calling.

God has gifted us all with some ability to bring in wealth. His word says, He gives us power to get wealth. What power has he entrusted into your hand. Can you bake, sew, sing, write, decorate, motivate, teach, etc.? What's in your hand? There is something that you can do.

Are you focused and driven about your assignment from the Lord?

Jesus was passionate about His assignment. He didn't allow anyone to get him off focus. He came to die for the sins of the world in order to reconcile man to God. He talked about it when he walked with the disciples. He talked about it when he ate with the disciples. It was his passion. He refused to be distracted even by those who sought his life. His assignment involved those who set themselves as enemies against him. He didn't abandon his task to get back at them. He kept his eyes on the cross. When we are passionate about what God has called

42

us to do, no one will be able to distract us from purpose. And we will be successful in this life.

Are you pursuing money?

Do not wear yourself out to get rich; have the wisdom to show restraint. Cast but a glance at riches, and they are gone, for they will surely sprout wings and fly off to the sky like an eagle. (Proverbs 23:4-5 NIV)

Be honest in answering this question. Are you seriously seeking His heart or his hand? To seek the heart of God is to seek His righteousness and His kingdom. To seek the hand of God is to seek after provision or money.

Understand money is **not** the root of all evil. The love of money and the pursuit of money is what God despises. Money should not become our god. Money is merely a tool for advancing the kingdom. If we seek after it, we won't be able to obtain it.

In St. Matthew 6:33 God tells us to seek first the Kingdom of God and His righteousness and our provision would be handled. We need not worry about what we will wear, eat, or drink. God promises that if we give attention to His Kingdom, he will take care of our every need. We will not know lack. So our basic needs will be covered if we are seeking His Kingdom first.

Are you a good steward?

The earth is the Lord's and the fullness thereof
and all that dwell therein. (Psalm 24:1)

Everything that we own belongs to God, not just the tithe. Every single thing. Your creativity, your body, your house, your car; it all belongs to God. He has blessed you.

43

A good steward will acknowledge the Lord about every disbursement; since all of it is his.

We buy expensive phones, gadgets, clothing, cars, jewelry, etc. Nothing is wrong with expensive purchases, except most of the time we haven't asked God if that's where He wants His money to go. It's all His money. Is this where he assigned it at this time? So we spend haphazardly and then are surprised when we don't have enough. We ought to acknowledge God in all our ways and let him direct our paths.

The category that Americans overspend the most in is food. We eat out far too often. We could be better managers of our bodies and our finances, if we prepared more of our own meals at home. What are we spending God's money on?

The Bible says that where our treasure is, there will be our hearts also. In other words, whatever we spend our money on, that's what we love. God wants to be our first love. So we can check our hearts by looking at our checkbooks. Is the majority of our money going to indulgences (cable, electronics, credit card purchases, hobbies, restaurants, entertainment, etc.)? Or is it going to fund the kingdom?

Our goal is that when we view our bank statements, we find that we are generous sowers in God's kingdom.

Certainly, the Lord wants us to be blessed and to have nice things. But everything must be in its proper season. Know what financial season you are in. If you have a mountain of debt, this is not a time to pursue lavish purchases. We are often overanxious. Most of us operate outside of our season. We bless ourselves and sorrow over it, when it's time to pay the bills.

> The blessings of the Lord maketh rich and
> he added no sorrow (Proverbs 10:22).

A wise steward does NOT live above his means or even at his means. **The wise steward lives below his means.**
You will never have wealth if you do not learn this important principle. Live below what you take in. Tally up all your income and all your expenses. If your expenses exceed your income, you must downsize. Cut out and cut down until what you spend is much less than what you bring in.

Keeping up with the proverbial Jones' will also affect your money flow. If your friends are going to dinner and the movies, it doesn't mean you can always tag along. Understand that you could be in different financial seasons or have different financial goals. Don't follow your friends into financial indebtedness. Your financial decisions should NOT be based upon what your friends are doing.

A good steward will operate from a spending plan. Know where you stand financially, and work well from a viable spending plan.

> Proverbs 27:23 says be thou diligent to
> know the state of thy flocks, and look well
> to thy herds.

Good stewardship also requires that one save for a rainy day. We all should have adequate savings. We teach our congregants to have **no less** than 2 savings accounts:
One short term account (min goal $1000) for car repairs, appliance and home repairs, etc. and one long term (min goal 8 months living expenses) for emergencies in case of job loss. Some people have college funds, vacation accounts and Christmas club savings, in addition to the 2 basic savings accounts.

Savings is important, but we can't stop there. Savings alone will not get us to the wealthy place. We absolutely must invest. Wisdom calls for us to invest for our future. Draw interest on your money. Cause it to multiply. We should have 401k's, IRA's, and other investment vehicles.

> Thou oughtest therefore to have put my money
> to the exchangers (bankers), and then at my
> coming I should have received mine own with
> usury (interest). Matthew 25:27

Research your investment options; but diligently seek God about **where** you should invest. Let him direct His money.

Are you a borrower?

Romans 13:8 says, "Owe no man anything."

It is not a sin to borrow. Our economy is set up in such a way that the average person finds it necessary to borrow in order to purchase a home, a car, or pursue higher education. There are other times, we find ourselves in a health crisis or other emergency, and we have no other recourse, but to borrow.

Nevertheless most Americans do not have the proper perspective toward borrowing. We see borrowing as an enormous "blessing" to get all the things we wouldn't normally be able to afford. We have misused and mishandled debt. As a result, our financial houses came crumbling down.

Credit is essentially borrowing from your future income. We take from tomorrow, today; when we haven't the slightest idea what tomorrow holds. Think about it: you are taking on a debt for which you promise to pay next year or within the next few years. So you begin those future years at a deficit. The proper mindset is to store up for tomorrow, not take from tomorrow. If we truly grasp this, we would use credit much more carefully.

God called you be a lender, not a borrower. In Deuteronomy 28, He said that we shall lend to many nations and not borrow.

If we want the wealth that God promised us, we should be reluctant to borrow. Our proper place, as a wealthy believer, is as a lender. Receiving pre-approved credit applications in the mail is not God's best promise for us. He wants us to live a debt-free life. God's Word says that the borrower is servant to the lender (Prov. 22:7). Let's work to shed our debt.

Do you pay those that you owe?

While it is not a sin to borrow, it is a sin to borrow and not return the item or pay the debt. The Bible says the wicked borrow and payeth not again (Psalm 37:21). We don't want to be named among the wicked. God requires His children to be just. When we do not pay our debts, it is very close to stealing.

We are expected to pay those that we owe. We shouldn't get angry or upset because a creditor calls to collect what you borrowed. Make every honest attempt to pay all those that you owe.

Do you sow cheerfully?

> Speak to the children of Israel, that they bring Me an offering. From everyone who gives it willingly with his heart you shall take My offering (Ex. 25:1-2).
>
> Every man according as he purposeth in his heart, so let him give, not grudgingly, or of

necessity: for God loveth a cheerful giver.
II Corinthians 9:7

He trusts you to give back to Him whenever He asks. At times, we get stingy. We hoard. We get possessive. When we drawback in this way, God cannot generously bless us.

Know that our God is a God of abundance. He does everything big. Two fish and five loaves fed a multitude of quite possibly over 15,000 (5,000 men plus women and children) and He still had 12 baskets left over.

When Peter and the disciples had toiled all night and caught no fish, Jesus showed up and told them to cast their nets on the other side. There were so many fish, the nets brake and they had to call for help.

God is in the overflow. He gets excited about blessing his children. But he wants his children to give like he gives – bountifully and cheerfully.

He gives seed to the sower. Are you sowing into the kingdom? If you sow cheerfully and generously, you shall reap in that same way.

Do you give to the poor?

> He that giveth unto the poor shall not lack:
> but he that hideth his eyes shall have
> many a curse. Proverbs 28:27

> He that hath pity upon the poor lendeth
> unto the Lord; and that which he hath giv-
> en will he pay him again. Proverbs 19:17

This last one is one of our favorite scriptures. Can you imagine, having God owe you? What a grand concept.

God will be no man's debtor. He will lavish us with his favor and blessings. He said that we would have the poor with us always. And He expects us to give to them. It's like an insurance policy. You give to the poor now and you insure that you will never be the poor.

So if we don't have the money, it's because we have left something undone. We must begin to move in purpose. Following these scriptures will cause us to possess all the wealth that God has assigned to us.

It is part of our assignment on earth to prosper and have wealth. So let's get our financial houses in order.

Chapter 8

Ain't No Stopping Us Now

When the Lord drops those witty ideas in your hearts, be aggressive about getting them to market, despite any impediment you may face. Most people give up way too soon. The minute they meet a blockage, they back up. Understand that your wealth is on the other side of that barrier and refuse to give up. Failure and poverty are not optional.

You must be convinced of your call. When your mind is made up, no one can stop you. You must become vigilant about the vision. Understand that your obedience may help to feed, heal, rescue, or clothe someone. This mindset should get you past any barriers that might present themselves.

We have all types of gifts in our hands. And many of them are underutilized or not used at all. God gave you gifts to bring in the wealth. We should understand that we have to have wealth in order to finish our course on the earth. It is important in the kingdom that God use you to meet the needs of others. We are most definitely blessed to be a blessing.

Whatever God has put in your heart, he gives you power to bring it forth. There are dreams and visions in all of our hearts. When a person decides to act on what God has told him to do, then God brings the provision to fund the vision.

The Bible tells us that without faith it is impossible to please God. You must have faith in God and His ability. It also says, "The trying of our faith worketh patience." And it's by faith and patience that we inherit the promises.

The trying of our faith represents trials, tribulations, and tests. When they are manifested in our lives, we have the awesome opportunity to receive the promise. The trial will get you to the promise or the wealth. It's the trial that caused you to come up with another way of doing something. It's the trial of losing your job that launched you into your own business. It's the tribulation of needing some widget that brings forth that invention.

So never stop at the trial. Don't sit down in front of the hurdle. When you go through the trial, holding on to your faith, you will get the promise. Someone is depending on you for their breakthrough. Your book may be the one that causes them to give their life to Christ. Your invention may give you the wealth to feed hungry children all over the world. It's not just about you. This thing is bigger than you.

Refuse to accept a defeatist attitude. In the past, we have given up, just at the brink of the promise. These are the obstacles that will keep us from getting where God has called us.

"I don't know where to go"	"I am too old"
"I am not licensed or certified"	"I don't have enough time"
"It's too hard"	"I am not smart enough"
"I don't have enough money"	"I don't feel like it"

Napoleon Hill said, "No one is ever defeated until he quits in his own mind." Let that resonate in your spirit. No one is ever defeated...until he quits in his mind or heart. So you are not defeated until you think that you are. So don't ever quit. Persevere.

Tribulation is always temporary. And on our way to destiny, we will meet challenges. We must learn how to get beyond them. We should look at the circumstances that arise as, a temporary inconvenience for the glory of God.

Every challenge that comes into our lives will eventually pass from our lives. Think about the trouble you've experienced in the past. Most of it, if not all of it is no longer current. The scriptures say it so eloquently, "And it came to pass." That blockage will eventually be removed or you will get around it.

The word crisis in Asian culture means opportunity. Therefore each crisis or setback comes into our lives is an opportunity to move closer to our destiny.

Dr. Mike Murdock says that everything we need is in someone else around us. We must tap into that someone. Don't be afraid to ask for assistance. There is someone who is willing and able to help you. Someone has the information that you need. Someone can give you a start. But don't wait on them. Do all that you can until God sends that person into your life. Not only that, but we'd like to say that what someone else needs is in you. You are the answer to someone else's problem. Sometimes as you are helping others, you get the help you need.

Do whatever it takes.

Refuse to allow poverty and failure to be options in your life. You must possess the wealth. There is no other option. If a challenge presents itself, learn how to get around it; because you refuse to live in lack. Refuse to live outside of purpose. God has made a way for you to escape the curse of poverty. If you follow His instructions, you cannot fail.

When you reach a roadblock on your way to the bank, you take an alternate route to get to your destination. That's the same thing you need to do on your way to destiny. Readjust so you can move forward in what God is calling you to do. Remember what God said. Keep that Word in your spirit. Don't take down. Press in. Don't back up or get angry.

Your trust must be in the Lord. He is Jehovah-Jireh. If you continually agree with God, you will never go back to that place of poverty.

Don't depend on any person or company. There was a time if you worked for "The Big 3 (Ford, GM, & Chrysler)," your job was secure. You did not have to worry about your financial future. That is no longer true. The auto industry has failed, along with the banks and many other corporations. They all looked to government to bail them out. As believers, we must depend on and look to God only. Do not depend on your job for your income. Hours are being cut: salaries, benefits and departments down-sized. Do not depend on anyone other than God to take care of you. Let no man determine your destiny. God has the plan to your remarkable future. Follow His plan.

What if your job goes out of business tomorrow, what would you do? Would you apply for unemployment? Would you apply for welfare? Do you have enough savings and investments to live? God has given you health and gifts. How will you use them?

Launch forth your business, invention, idea, or book that God has given you. Don't wait until you are forced to do something. Don't allow a pink slip to move you into action.

Begin today. Let the witty invention or idea that God has given you, work for you.

Wealth is a state of mind. Is it in you, yet? There are a number of wealthy men and women that at some point lost their wealth; but because of their mindset they were able to regain it.

God has given you so many ideas. You have so much in your hands. What are you going to do to fund the kingdom?

If we avail ourselves, God will put things around us and put in us the information that we need to be successful. Read. Search the web. Ask a friend.

God has put something in your heart to increase your wealth. The Bible says "He works in us the will and the do of His good pleasure." These things that we desire to do are put in our thoughts by God. And it's your job to turn your thoughts into wealth.

It's time to be about your Father's business. Think about Joseph how he stored up for Pharaoh. People came from all over in the time of famine. Because of God's wisdom entrusted to Joseph, God transferred the wealth to Israel. The Israelites were able to spoil the Egyptians. God will put into the hands of those that are willing to put it back into the kingdom. He gives to those who give back to Him.

The pipe gets wet as the water flows through it. God loves mankind. He says I am good to the just and unjust. He wants to use his agents that he placed in the earth so we can be the pipe that he funnels his resources through. We get wet, too. God has given you a gift, a dream or a vision. So he can use you to fund His covenant.

There is great wealth in the earth. Extract it. We can all have the life that God wants us to have. According to our faith, be it unto us. We live in one of the wealthiest countries in the world. All the gold still has not been dis-covered. People buy and trade here every day. We live in a time where you can trade internationally, from your living room. There is so much money yet to be made. Certainly, there are talks of famine (recessions and depressions). But don't let the bad news fool you. There is plenty of money available. Don't let people talk you out of the vision. People will buy and they will fund the vision. Even in the midst of a struggling economy, restaurant parking lots are still full.

Be passionate about this thing. Be committed. It is no longer an option, to stay in the financial position that you are in. God has entrusted you with your gift or talent. You can't afford to sit on it. So the time is now.

Chapter 9

Who Wants To Be A Millionaire?

You must not look at this extreme makeover as some type of get rich quick scheme. In fact, it's not about getting rich. It's about getting riches to advance the kingdom of God. Don't set your heart on getting rich. Set your heart on advancing the Kingdom.

We must have a balanced approach to the financial side of wealth. The scriptures warn us that riches are a snare. If we look closely at what Jesus had to say to his disciples, we can get a better picture. "I tell you the truth; it is hard for a rich man to enter the kingdom of heaven" Matthew 19:23. In fact, He said, that it is easier for a camel to go through the eye of a needle than for a rich man to enter the kingdom of God. The Lord wants us all to consider that scripture. Don't gloss over it. Or dismiss it as if it doesn't apply to you.

Jesus was using his own language to communicate the near impossibility of salvation for anyone possessed by material wealth. So he used the largest animal and the smallest opening his audience knew. He was showing that the rich man that is attached to his riches cannot enter the kingdom. It is the man or woman that wears his riches as a loose garment, who will be able to enter the kingdom of God.

We have all witnessed our own brothers and sisters fall prey to this very word. These anointed men and women of God sacrificed their intimacy with the Lord on the altar of Mammon (Money as a god).

They didn't start out that way.

They started out sincere and trustworthy, giving their all for the cause of Christ; much like the rich young ruler. When he asked Jesus, "What lack I yet?" Jesus pointed him to the commandments. He responded, "I have kept these from my youth." You see, he started out with the right spirit.

So, what happened? When Jesus said, give it all up, he couldn't. He walked away sorrowful. The money had him.

Mammon is a god. And there is no way to serve both gods. The Lord requires that we put nothing before Him. Money should not have us. We should have it. Somehow some of us have lost sight of its proper place in our lives. Many Christian leaders have fallen prey to its enticement and lost their spiritual inheritance. Mark 8:36 says, "What would it profit a man to gain the whole world and lose his soul?" There is absolutely no benefit.

It is important that we don't get fooled into thinking that it can't happen to us. The Bible warns us to not think that we can't fall, because that it is when we can.

> "Wherefore let him that thinketh he
> standeth take heed lest he fall"
> 1Corinthians 10:12.

You **can** fall just like those who have gone before you. Walk circumspectly. Give generously. Everything we get belongs to God. We are his managers. If He says, "Sell everything and follow me." We must do so, and without hesitation.

Christian entrepreneur and philanthropist, Arch Bonnema is a man who loves God. Since 1991, he and his wife, Sherry, have tithed a minimum of 50 percent of their finances and work hours to missions. They've partnered with local ministries in Uganda, Kenya, India, and Ethiopia

58

to build orphan homes centered around churches and to staff them with widows, explicitly following the words of James 1:27 (which are etched inside his home).

Their decision to give 50% came after the two had attended a missions' conference. As they were headed home, Arch told his wife he had been feeling like they ought to increase their commitment from 35% to 50%. His wife, Sherry, replied with enthusiasm that God had been telling her that for months. She was just waiting on her husband for confirmation. Their decision to tithe lavishly was followed by the loss of their savings and other assets, just about everything, except their home. They even sold their last car, a 2-year-old Cadillac, so they could keep the pledges they had made to ministries. They gave everything they had, including cashing in their retirement, to make sure that their promises to missions were fulfilled. His income dropped while his giving increased, percentage-wise. No problem, they thought. They just sold everything. They didn't feel they needed it anyway. It was more important to the Bonnemas that they fulfilled their commitment to God.

It wasn't until they had given away pretty much everything they had over a span of six years when, all of a sudden, everything just reversed. Bonnema said, "God started building my businesses faster than I ever could have imagined. Within two years I had more money than I ever had in my whole life." (Adapted from Articlesnatch.com written by Julie Lyons)

Money didn't have Arch or Sherry Bonnema. They had it. When we are able to release it for the cause of Christ, God can trust us. He trusts those that trust Him.

Our focus must not be on getting rich.

As your finances increase, put accountability measures in

place. Keep your vision before you. Bonnema etched it on the ceiling of his home (James 1:27). Increase your time in prayer and study of the Word. Place people around yourself who will challenge you in righteous living. They should be people you admire and respect.

Most importantly, humble yourself before the Lord by consistently attacking pride in your heart. Be sober, be vigilant, be aware of the tentacles that money can have. Don't allow it to get its hooks in you. Put no confidence in your own sinful flesh.

Let your focus continually be on the Kingdom of Heaven. Everything else pales in comparison.

Chapter 10

LET THE TRANSFORMATION BEGIN

Now that you know what is lacking in your life. It's time to begin the transformation. The next 30 days are key to your success. Don't delay, start now. You don't have to wait until the first day of the month. Begin today. In 30 days you will be closer to the new you. This thirty day makeover plan will begin the process. It does not end there. Continue to develop the person that God wants you to become. This 30 day plan is simply a jumpstart. It will take years to get where you need to be. Don't get discouraged. You will see results sooner than you think.

Before you begin, ask God to reveal your purpose. Know what it is that you are called to do. How does God want you to advance his kingdom?

Secondly, repent of **all** sin. Sin clogs our ability to hear God. The Bible says, "He that knoweth to do good and doeth it not, to him it is sin." If you have not consistently paid tithes and offerings, commit to paying, regularly. If you have been lacking in your walk, it's time to do all that you know to do. Leave nothing undone.

Develop the work that He has given you. Whether it's a book, ministry, invention, cd project, or business, start working on it day one. Spend some time everyday developing your idea. Make sure you take time to rest on the Sabbath.

Begin with a 30 day media fast. Cut off the television. Use the computer for work and Bible study purposes only. Cut out all extra-curricular activities that require spending money for these 30 days. Every day (except your Sabbath) work on the idea that God has given you. Take a walk or jog every day. Get your exercise in. Begin the journey to your makeover.

Now let the transformation begin.

30 Day Wealth Plan

Day 1: Focus on Forgiveness. Make amends with those with which you have offenses. Choose to forgive. Bitterness and anger clog your pipe. They stagnate your creative flow. Write out the offenses on a sheet of paper. Pray over them and release them to the Lord. Tear up the paper as an act of forgiveness. Continue in a spirit of forgiveness.

Day 2: Prepare a menu for the month. Change your eating habits. Avoid fried and fatty foods. Add one extra glass of water to your daily diet. Week 2 add 2 extra glasses. Week 3 add 3 extra glasses and so on until you get to 8 glasses. Eliminate processed and much of the junk food from your diet.

Day 3: Do Good. Do something nice for a person who has hurt you (present or past). Send a letter, email or card.

Day 4: Prepare a spending plan or budget. Cut expenses. Live beneath your means. Figure out all your debt. Prepare a plan to attack the debt. Your goal is to become debt-free. Make arrangements to pay off your debt. Don't worry if it will take some years to dig yourself out. It took years to get yourself in. If you stick to the plan you will get out much faster.

Day 5: Help a widow or the elderly. Offer some type of service. Pick up prescriptions, mow lawn, go to the store, or drive them to their doctor's appointment.

Day 6: Start saving your coins every day. At the end of

everyday empty your pockets into a jar or bottle. Every time you get extra money, after you pay tithes and offerings, put half toward your debt and half toward savings.

Day 7: Write down all the things for which you are thankful. Praise the Lord for his faithfulness to you.

Day 8: Get your life in order. Set a schedule to implement your ideas. Include ministry, work, and volunteer opportunities. Also include a Sabbath day. Keep to your schedule. You will find yourself to be much more productive.

Day 9: Call a family member or friend that you haven't talked to in a while. Encourage and pray with him/her.

Day 10: Collect bottles, newspapers and cans for recycling. Prepare proper containers to store them in to keep order. Do something good for the earth.

Day 11: Clear out your garage and/or basement. Collect items for a garage sale or put on Ebay, Craigslist, etc. Host the sale within the next week or so. Whatever hasn't sold, if it's not junk, donate to a shelter. Put half the money towards your debt and half towards your savings.

Day 12: Open up 2 savings accounts: one for short-term savings and one for long-term savings. Be committed to put in 10% every pay period. If that is not possible, put in 5%. Split that 5% between both accounts. Never skip adding to your savings acct. Work your way up to putting in the 10%.

Tithes and offerings come first and then add to your savings.

Day 13: Study the scriptures on giving.

Day 14: Comparison shop for insurances: auto, life, health, and homeowners (or renters). Reduce your costs. If possible, increase your deductible. Put away savings to cover the larger deductible.

Day 15: Help out at a homeless shelter. Donate food to feed the hungry. Pray for those that are less fortunate than you. Be thankful to God for the many blessings that you have.

Day 16: Reduce your food costs. Work out a plan to spend less on groceries. Eliminate prepared foods, restaurant and fast food meals. Cut coupons. Find a less expensive grocery store in your area.

Day 17: Keep your word. Fulfill a promise that you've neglected. Apologize for the delay.

Day 18: Go through your closets. Organize them. Rid yourself of all the clothing and shoes that you no longer use. Donate it to a shelter or mission. Make sure that they are in usable condition. Keep receipts for tax purposes.

Day 19: Place motivational reading materials (on finance, faith, and/or purpose) and a Bible in your bathroom, car and family room.

Day 20: Find an unnecessary expense in your budget and work on cutting it out all together.

Day 21: Visit someone sick or in the hospital. Pray for them

Day 22: Clean out your car including the trunk of your car. Give away those things that you can no longer use. Don't use your car as storage space for your home. You should make sure that you have a spare tire, tire iron, jumper cables, and an emergency road kit. If you carry a blanket or towel in your trunk, put it in a plastic storage bag (not garbage bag) to protect it.

Day 23: Be kind to a stranger.

Day 24: Rotate and balance tires for better gas mileage.

Day 25: Send a 'thinking of you' note to your parents and grandparents. Let them know that you love them.

Day 26: Reduce your cable bill. By now, you should realize that you really don't need it. So cut down your plan.

Day 27: Donate items to an orphanage. Call ahead to find out their needs. It may be books, toiletries, school supplies, etc. Maybe get another family to participate in this. You can split the costs. In lieu of finances, you can also donate a service. Give a talk, read a story, serve in some other capacity.

Day 28: Cash in bottles and cans. Put the money with coins that you are saving daily.

Day 29: Release someone who owes you a debt but can't afford to pay it back.

Day 30: Get coin wrappers and wrap the loose change that you've saved. Deposit it into the savings account of your choice.

For the next 30 days continue to maintain what you have established. Repeat the repeatable sections of the 30 day plan each month. Work on your idea 6 days a week.

Create a dream board or dream book. Include what you want to accomplish in the next 5 to 10 years. A dream book is a scrap book that you create using newspapers and magazines. A dream board is a collage. You cut out pictures and words that symbolize your visions and goals. You can use markers as well.

The purpose is to be able to visualize your dreams and to keep a tangible representation of that vision close at hand. It keeps you inspired and maintains your focus. Pray and develop a detailed marketing plan for your idea. Work the plan and keep moving forward.

Other books written by Oscar and Crystal Jones

When The Vow Breaks

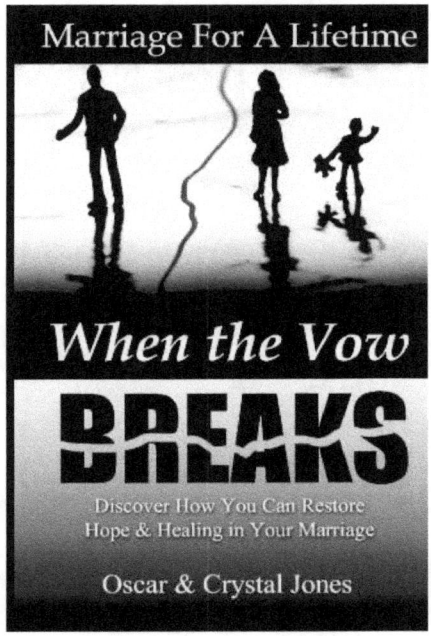

ISBN: 145054214X

No Longer A Dream

ISBN: 1452828334

Newlywed Handbook

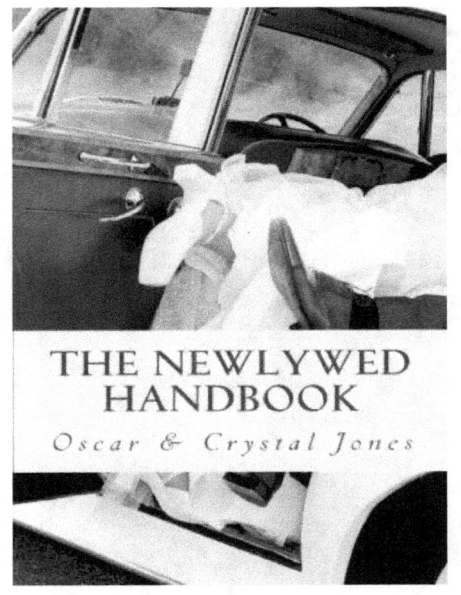

ISBN: 1452847126

Restore The Roar

ISBN:9781456353759

www.ingramcontent.com/pod-product-compliance
Lightning Source LLC
Chambersburg PA
CBHW071306170526
45165CB00003B/1438